Georgia, My State
Geographic Regions

Piedmont

by Doraine Bennett

STATE STANDARDS PUBLISHING®

Your State • Your Standards • Your Grade Level

Dear Educators, Librarians and Parents . . .

Thank you for choosing the *"Georgia, My State"* Series! We have designed this series to support the Georgia Department of Education's Georgia Performance Standards for elementary level Georgia studies. Each book in the series has been written at appropriate grade level as measured by the ATOS Readability Formula for Books (Accelerated Reader), the Lexile Framework for Reading, and the Fountas & Pinnell Benchmark Assessment System for Guided Reading. Photographs and/or illustrations, captions, and other design elements have been included to provide supportive visual messaging to enhance text comprehension. Glossary and Word Index sections introduce key new words and help young readers develop skills in locating and combining information.

We wish you all success in using the *"Georgia, My State"* Series to meet your student or child's learning needs. For additional sources of information, see www.georgiaencyclopedia.org.

Jill Ward, President

Publisher
State Standards Publishing, LLC
1788 Quail Hollow
Hamilton, GA 31811
USA
1.866.740.3056
www.statestandardspublishing.com

Library of Congress Cataloging-in-Publication Data
Bennett, Doraine, 1953-
    Piedmont / by Doraine Bennett.
        p. cm. -- (Georgia, my state. Geographic Regions)
    Includes index.
    ISBN-13: 978-1-935077-22-0 (hardcover)
    ISBN-10: 1-935077-22-8 (hardcover)
    ISBN-13: 978-1-935077-27-5 (pbk.)
    ISBN-10: 1-935077-27-9 (pbk.)
    1. Georgia--Juvenile literature. 2. Georgia--Geography--Juvenile literature. I. Title.
F286.3.B466 2009
917.58'4--dc22
                                        2009013009

Table of Contents

The red clay sometimes makes the rivers look muddy.

Appalachian Plateau

Blue Ridge

Valley and Ridge

Piedmont

Upper Coastal Plain

Lower Coastal Plain

There are lots of rolling hills in the Piedmont.

4

Let's Explore!

Hi, I'm Bagster! Let's explore the Piedmont **geographic region**. A region is an area named for the way the land is formed. Piedmont means *foot of the mountains*. Rolling hills cover this region. The soil is mostly red clay. It stains clothes and shoes. It sometimes makes rivers look muddy.

An artist carved faces into Stone Mountain!

This Mountain has Faces!

Large chunks of rock lie under the Piedmont soil. This rock layer is called **bedrock**. Sometimes the soil washes away. The rock sticks out of the ground. **Stone Mountain** is a large piece of the bedrock. People come here to see the faces carved in Stone Mountain.

Atlanta is the capital of Georgia.

Can you find the capitol building?

Our State Capital

Atlanta is the state **capital** of Georgia. It is in the Piedmont region. A state capital is a city where the government of a state is located. Georgia's laws are made in the **capitol** building. Atlanta is the largest city in Georgia. Careful, we might get caught in a traffic jam!

The Cherokee Indians lived near the mountains.

Creek Indians lived in the river valleys.

Which Indians Lived Here?

Both Creek and Cherokee Indians lived in the Piedmont. The Creeks lived in the river valleys. The Cherokees lived farther north, near the **Blue Ridge Mountains**.

President Roosevelt could not walk.

He believed the water at Warm Springs made his legs stronger.

Warm Water from the Ground

Warm water flows from the ground at **Warm Springs**. The water is heated deep inside the earth. Many people believed the warm water helped heal sickness. President Franklin Roosevelt came to soak in the water. He could not walk. He believed the water helped make his legs stronger.

The land drops steeply at the fall line. Water flows fast.

The Piedmont ends at the fall line.

What is the Fall Line?

The Piedmont ends at the **fall line**. The land drops steeply here. Rivers flow faster over the steep land. There are **rapids** where the water flows very fast. There are also waterfalls where the water falls down over rocks.

The Masters Golf Tournament is played in Augusta. It's famous!

People in Macon have a Cherry Blossom Festival each year.

The Springer Opera House is in Columbus. It is the State Theater of Georgia.

Which Cities Are on the Fall Line?

Boats bringing people and supplies up Georgia rivers stopped at the fall line. They could not go over the rapids and waterfalls. People built cities where the boats stopped. They built **Columbus** on the **Chattahoochee River**. They built **Macon** on the **Ocmulgee River**. They built **Augusta** on the **Savannah River**.

It's fun to swim in the lake. Jump in!

Water backs up behind the dam. It makes a lake.

Let's Swim!

Georgia did not always have big lakes. People built **dams** on some rivers. The dams blocked the water. It backed up behind the dams and made lakes. The dams and lakes help prevent floods. They provide water for nearby cities. They also help make electricity. The lakes are good places to swim! Jump in!

It's fun to ride on the lake! Hold on tight!

Lake Lanier looks like this from an airplane. It is the largest lake in Georgia.

Let's Ride on the Water!

Georgia's largest lake is in the Piedmont region. It is called **Lake Lanier**. Lake Lanier was made by a dam on the Chattahoochee River. It is almost half as big as the city of Atlanta!

Hold on tight! Let's ride across Lake Lanier!

Glossary

Atlanta – The state capital of Georgia. Atlanta is the largest city in Georgia.

Augusta – A city at the fall line on the Savannah River.

bedrock – A large layer of rock that lies under the soil in the Piedmont.

Blue Ridge Mountains – The chain of mountains in Georgia's Blue Ridge region.

capital – A city where the government of a state is located.

capitol – The building where laws are made.

Chattahoochee River – A river that flows through Columbus, Georgia.

Columbus – A city at the fall line on the Chattahoochee River.

dams – Concrete walls built on rivers to control the water flow.

fall line – A line of land across Georgia where the bedrock meets the coastal plain.

geographic region – An area named for the way the land is formed.

Lake Lanier – The largest lake in Georgia.

Macon – A city at the fall line on the Ocmulgee River.

Ocmulgee River – A river that flows through Macon, Georgia.

rapids – Water in a river that flows fast downhill.

Savannah River – A river that flows through Augusta, Georgia.

Stone Mountain – A large piece of bedrock that sticks out of the ground.

Warm Springs – A town known for its warm spring water.

Word Index

Image Credits

About the Author

Doraine Bennett has a degree in professional writing from Columbus State University in Columbus, Georgia, and has been writing and teaching writing for over twenty years. She has authored numerous articles in magazines for both children and adults and is the editor of the National Infantry Association's *Infantry Bugler* magazine. Doraine enjoys reading and writing books and articles for children. She lives in Georgia with her husband, Cliff.